D1459774

Mighty Bots

MEDICAL ROBOTS

THOMAS KINGSLEY TROUPE

WORLD BOOK

This World Book edition of *Medical Robots*
is published by agreement between
Black Rabbit Books and World Book, Inc.
© 2018 Black Rabbit Books,
2140 Howard Dr. West,
North Mankato, MN 56003 U.S.A.
World Book, Inc.,
180 North LaSalle St., Suite 900,
Chicago, IL 60601 U.S.A.

Jennifer Besel, editor; Grant Gould, interior designer; Michael Sellner,
cover designer; Omay Ayres, photo researcher

Library of Congress Control Number: 2016049962

ISBN: 978-0-7166-9331-4

Printed in the United States at CG Book Printers,
North Mankato, Minnesota, 56003. 3/17

Image Credits
Alamy: age fotostock: 4–5; flickr.
com/photos/uscviterbi/: USC Viterbi
School of Engineering, 9; Getty Images: The
Asahi Shimbun, 10; Bloomberg, 15, 27 (TUG); Frank
Perry, 12–13; iStock: eternalcreative, 26; Vladyslav Otsiat-
sia, 28 (doctor); National Geographic Creative: DMITRI AL-
EXANDER, 22; Newscom: Colin Anderson, 28 (background);
FRANCK ROBICHON, 16; Science Source: Science Picture
Co, Cover; Shutterstock: Andrii Vodolazhskyi, 27 (nanobots);
Chakrapong Zyn, 32; chombosan, 17; decade3d - anatomy
online, 18–19; ktsdesign, 20; Lightspring, 3, 21; Ociacia, 1,
31, Back Cover; Wire_man, 6–7; www.besticinc.com: Bestic
AB, 24, 25
Every effort has been made to contact copyright hold-
ers for material reproduced in this book. Any
omissions will be rectified in subsequent
printings if notice is given to the
publisher.

CONTENTS

CHAPTER 1

A Helping ROBOT

A man lies on the operating table. Steady robotic arms work on his heart. Nearby, a doctor controls the robot's movements. Together, the doctor and the robot save the man's life.

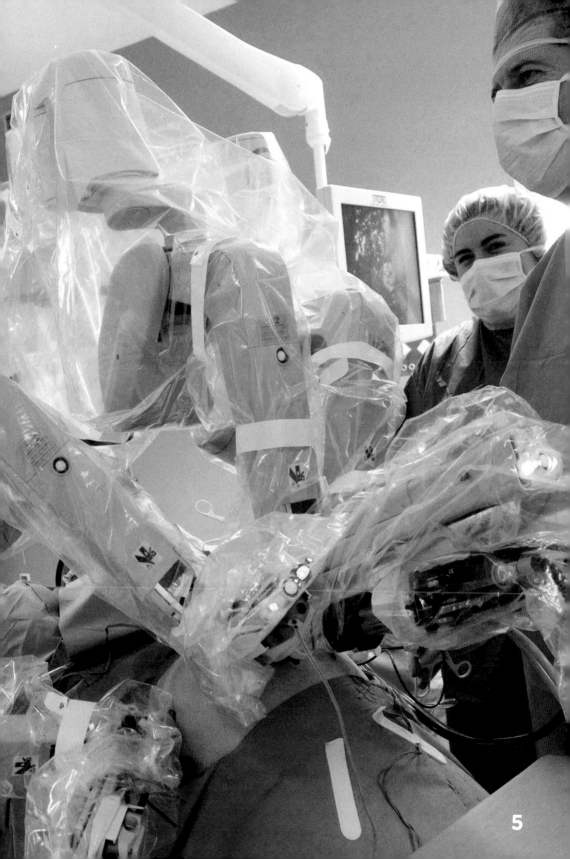

Medical Machines

Around the world, doctors use robots. Medical robots help in **surgeries**. Other robots deliver medical supplies. Tiny robots even travel in human blood.

CHAPTER 2

Built for Working with PEOPLE

Some robots work with **patients**. Bandit does exercises with people. It asks them to copy its movements. If they mess up, the robot corrects them. Bandit also encourages people to work harder.

How Big Is ·····▶ Bandit?

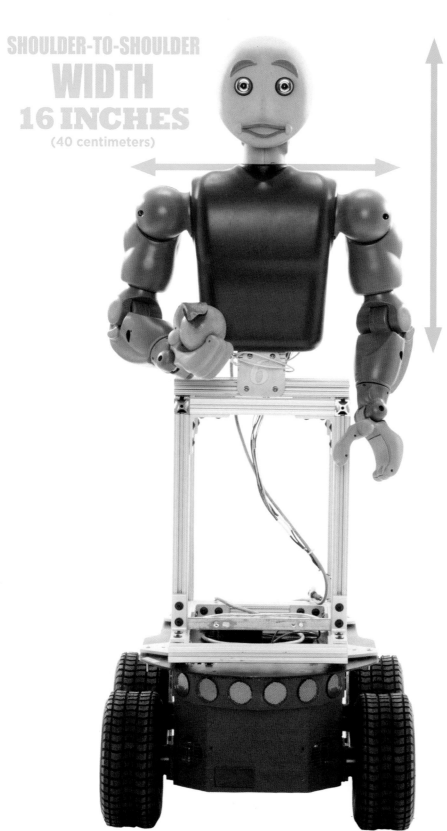

SHOULDER-TO-SHOULDER
WIDTH
16 INCHES
(40 centimeters)

HEIGHT
22 INCHES
(56 cm)

9

Hospital Helper

Robots can help hospital patients.
Cody is a robot that opens doors and
drawers. It reaches things for patients
in wheelchairs.

◄ • • • RIBA looks like a teddy bear.
This robot can lift patients out
of beds.

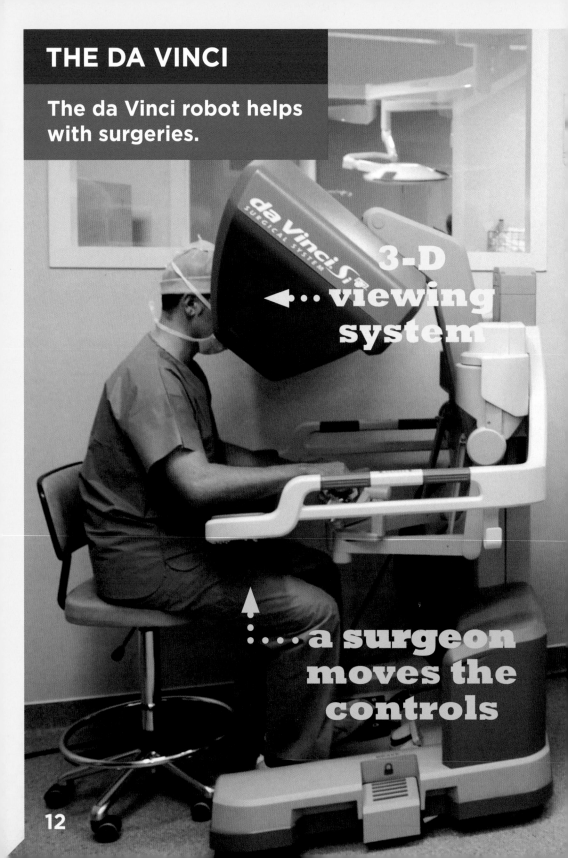

THE DA VINCI

The da Vinci robot helps with surgeries.

3-D ←⋯ viewing system

⋯ a surgeon moves the controls

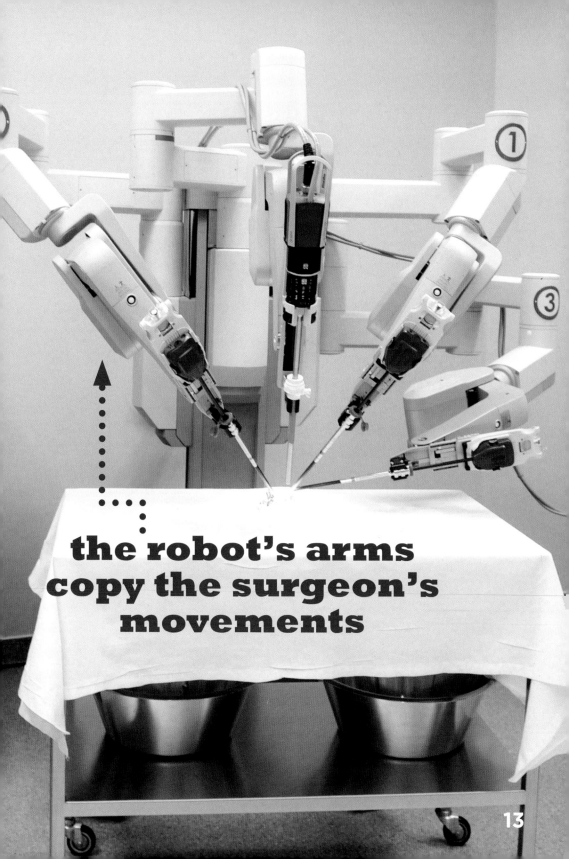

the robot's arms
copy the surgeon's
movements

Carrying Supplies

Medical robots come in all shapes and sizes. Some perform surgeries. Others deliver supplies and medicine.

The TUG is a box-shaped helper robot. It's **programmed** to move around a hospital. It brings supplies to doctors.

Sensors on the robot stop it from bumping into people.

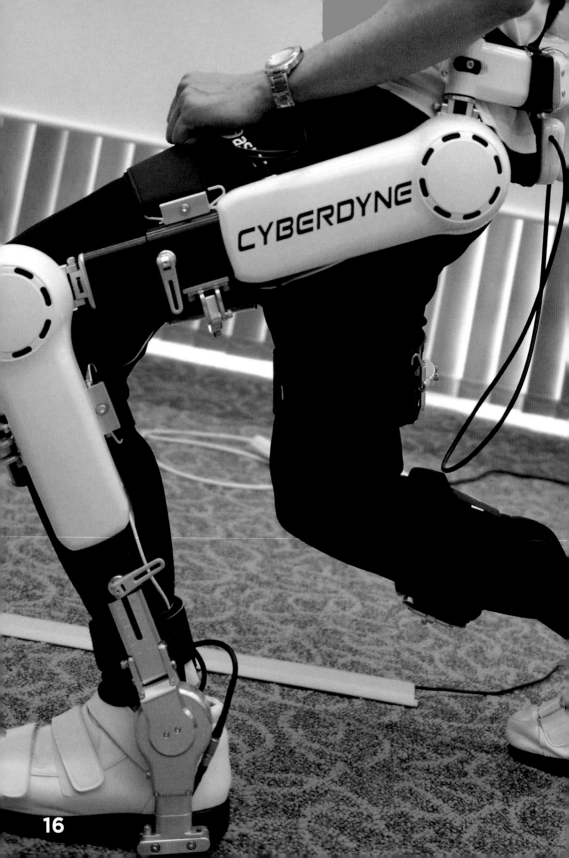

CHAPTER 3

Wired, Wearable
ROBOTS

Scientists have created robotic body parts too. Robotic legs help people walk. Ankle and knee **motors** adjust to a person's thoughts and movements. These adjustments help the leg walk naturally.

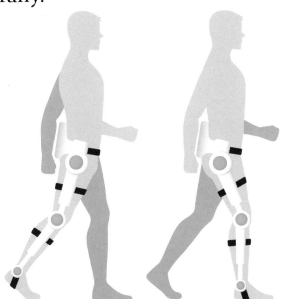

Argus II
bionic eye
helps blind people see light

BIONIC BODY
Scientists have created many different robotic body parts.

bionic ear
helps deaf people hear

nanobots
clear arteries

BiOM Ankle
powered ankle helps
people walk

bionic hand
senses touch

Bloodstream Battles

Some robots are very tiny. Nanobots move inside human bodies. Some clear blocked arteries. Others deliver medicine.

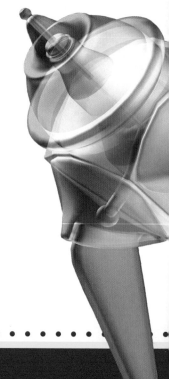

Some nanobots can find and kill cancer in people.

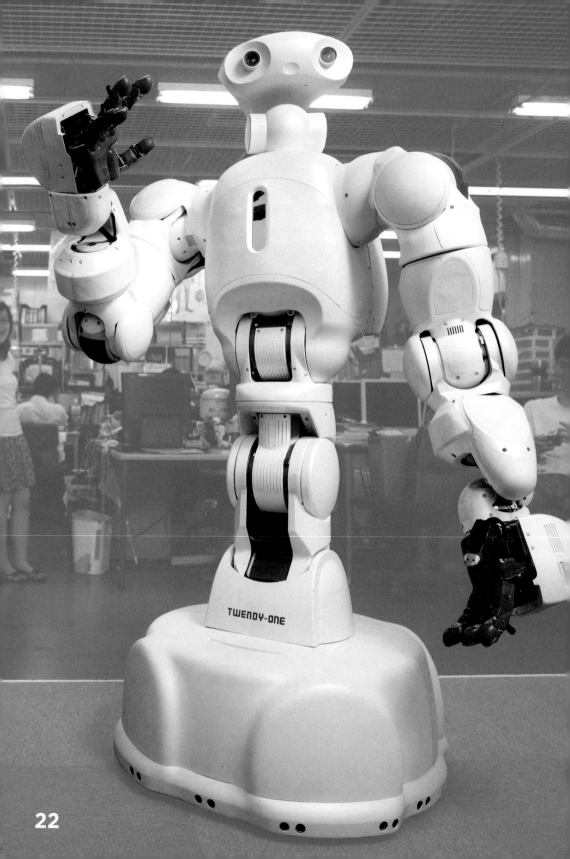

CHAPTER 4

HELPING Humans

Scientists are working to improve medical robots. Someday, a robot called Terapio will help nurses in a hospital. It will alert them to any problems. Other robots, such as

◀ • • • Twendy-One, will help elderly people with daily tasks.

Helping Humans Get Better Faster

Bestic is a robotic arm. The arm sits on a table. With the push of a button, the arm spoons up food. Bestic helps feed people who can't eat on their own.

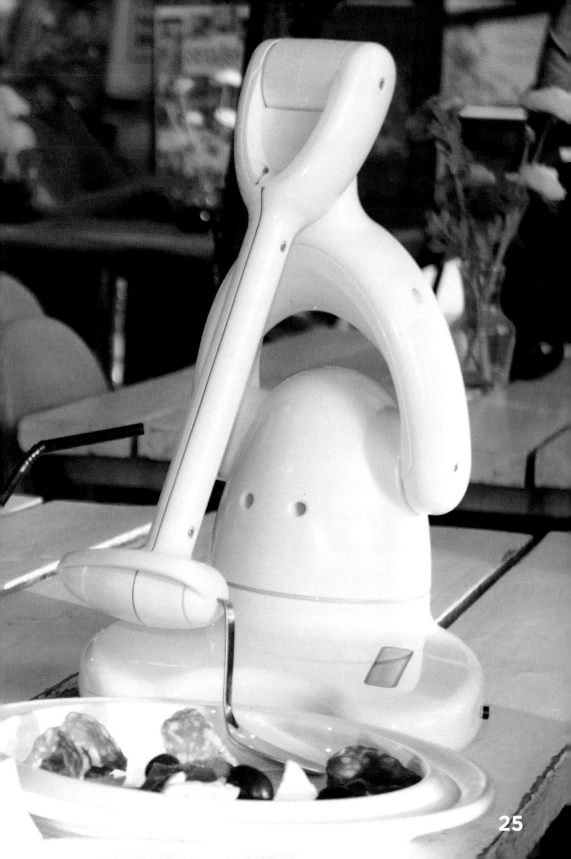

By the Numbers

more than
3 MILLION

number of patients treated
with da Vinci robots

estimated cost for one Argus II bionic eye

$

ABOUT
145,000

$4.2 BILLION

estimated amount spent worldwide on medical robots in 2015

1,000
pounds
(454 kilograms)

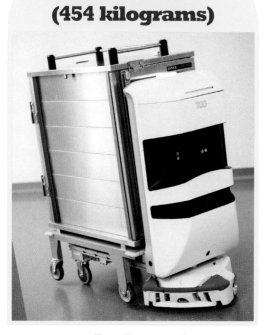

weight the TUG can pull

about

3
billion
number of nanobots that fit in a teaspoon

Future of Robo Health Care

Robots can't care for people on their own yet. They still need humans to program them. No one knows what future medical robots will look like. But they will continue to help people.

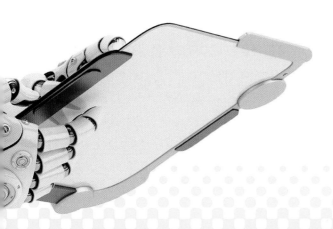

GLOSSARY

artery (AHR-tuh-ree)—a tube that carries blood from the heart to a body part

bionic (bi-AH-nik)—having body parts made strong or more capable by electronic devices

motor (MO-tur)—a machine that produces motion or power

patient (PAY-shunt)—a person getting medical care or treatment

program (PROH-gram)—to give a machine instructions to perform an action

sensor (SEN-sor)—a device that detects heat, light, sound, motion, or other things

surgeon (SUR-juhn)—a doctor who cuts into someone's body to fix something

surgery (SUR-juh-ree)—a medical treatment where a doctor cuts into someone's body to fix something

BOOKS

Faust, Daniel R. *Medical Robots*. Robots and Robotics. New York: PowerKids Press, 2017.

Mooney, Carla. *Wearable Robots*. Tech Bytes. Chicago: Norwood House Press, 2017.

Swanson, Jennifer. *National Geographic Kids. Everything Robotics: All the Robotic Photos, Facts, and Fun!* Everything Series. Washington, D.C.: National Geographic, 2016.

WEBSITES

Robotics
kidsahead.com/subjects/1-robotics

Robotics: Facts
idahoptv.org/sciencetrek/topics/robots/facts.cfm

Robots for Kids
www.sciencekids.co.nz/robots.html

INDEX